GOING

A HEALTHY GUIDE
TO MAKING THE SWITCH

VEGAN

by Dana Meachen Rau

COMPASS POINT BOOKS
a capstone imprint

Compass Point Books
1710 Roe Crest Drive
North Mankato, MN 56003

Acknowledgments
Special thanks to Alyssa Moskites, Greg Person, and my
new friends at Fire and Spice, for sharing their stories with me.

Editor: Jeni Wittrock
Designer: Sarah Bennett
Media Researcher: Svetlana Zhurkin
Production Specialist: Danielle Ceminsky

This book was manufactured with paper containing
at least 10 percent post-consumer waste.

Library of Congress Cataloging-in-Publication Data
Rau, Dana Meachen, 1971-
Going vegan : a healthy guide to making the switch / by Dana Meachen Rau.
     p. cm.
  Summary: "Describes the benefits, challenges, and steps to switching to a
vegan diet"—Provided by publisher.
  Includes bibliographical references and index.
  ISBN 978-0-7565-4521-5 (library binding)
  ISBN 978-0-7565-4529-1 (paperback)
  1. Veganism—Juvenile literature. I. Title.
  TX392.R38 2012
  613.2'622—dc23   2011043568

Image Credits: Alamy: Doug Steley B., 39; Capstone Studio: Karon Dubke,
cover, 9, 23, 35, 51, 59; Corbis: Caterina Bernardi, 56–57, Golden Pixels/Matt
Hess, 42–43; Dreamstime: Eric Wagner, 22 (bottom), Mangostock, 33, Monkey
Business Images, 30, Stockstudios, 34; Getty Images: Thomas Grass, 44–45,
Yellow Dog Productions, 46–47; iStockphoto: Factoria Singular, 40, George Peters,
24–25, Izvorinka Jankovic, 48–49, Steve Debenport, 28–29; Newscom: Andersen
Ross Cultura, 50, picture-alliance/Chromorange/Hans Miglbauer, 14–15, Richard
B. Levine, 6–7; Shutterstock: Bart Everett, 21, Diego Cervo, 41, duel, 12–13, Dusan
Zidar, 27, Edhar, 58, Francis Wong Chee Yen, 55, George Dolgikh, 7 (top right),
Hannamariah, 4–5, homeros, 18–19, Igor Dutina, 28 (top left), 31, Ildi Papp, 38,
Ivonne Wierink, 32, Konstantin L., 16–17, Marco Mayer, 42 (left), Mny-Jhee, 22
(top), Oliko, 47 (top right), oriori, 13 (top right), Picsfive, 15 (inset), pixelpeter,
10–11, Tatiana Gladskikh, 52–53, Tom Grundy, 20, vnlit, 54, Yuri Arcurs, 36–37;
USDA: ARS/Scott Bauer, 18

Visit Compass Point Books on the Internet at *www.capstonepub.com*.

Printed in the United States of America in North Mankato, Minnesota.
102011   006405CGS12

CONTENTS

CHAPTER ONE

EATING THOUGHTFULLY

AS A TEENAGER YOU HAVE PLENTY TO DO. There's not always time to sit down to dinner. A fast-food restaurant sometimes does the trick. Around almost every corner, you can find a place to stop for a quick meal.

The menu above the fast-food counter lists lots of options—hamburgers, double-bacon cheeseburgers, beef tacos, fried chicken, and chicken nuggets. If you go to a deli, you can choose from ham, roast beef, or turkey stuffed in a grinder roll and topped with bacon or cheese.

But what if you don't want to eat meat? You'll have to do a little more searching. Somewhere on the menu, there may be a salad or a baked potato. You can put veggies on a deli sandwich. But non-meat items are not a fast-food specialty. Your choices will be limited if you're not in the mood for meat.

Instead of cooking burgers and fries, some food trucks serve vegan fare to hungry customers.

Instead of quick stops and rushed meals, take a moment to think first. You may discover other restaurants in the area that serve foods to go. They may not have huge signs at the shopping mall or lining the highway. They may be quietly tucked down a side street or squeezed between bigger stores. It's worth seeking them out.

Fire and Spice is a restaurant in Hartford, Connecticut. Walk in the door, and you'll find a variety of fast food. There's Cajun tempeh, barbequed tofu, curried potatoes, vegetable stew, and steamed kale. There are drinks made of hibiscus flowers and ginger root. You can have brown rice or quinoa on the side.

There are even vegetable burgers and sweet potato fries. What makes this food different? It's all vegan.

BEYOND VEGETARIANISM

Vegetarians have decided to cut meat out of their diets. That includes all animal flesh—red meat (beef, pork, veal, lamb, and game), poultry, fish, and shellfish. Some vegetarians take it to the next step. Vegans are vegetarians who have decided to give up all animal products. That means meat of any kind. It also means the eggs that come from chickens and the milk that comes from cows.

Basic Foods Vegans Avoid

Red meat (beef, pork, veal, lamb, and game)

Poultry

Fish and shellfish

Dairy foods (milk, yogurt, cheese, and ice cream)

Eggs

FURTHER FOOD INGREDIENTS VEGANS MAY AVOID

Carmine/Cochineal (a red dye that comes from beetles)

Casein (a milk protein)

Gelatin (made from animal by-products)

Honey (from bees)

Lactose (a sugar found in milk)

Monoglycerides (from animal fat)

Rennet (enzyme from the stomach of calves, young goats, and sheep)

Whey (from milk)

There are even more food additives, dyes, vitamins, and ingredients that are animal based. Check online sources for more comprehensive lists.

Vegans abstain from other animal products too. You may not realize it, but when you're munching on a marshmallow, you're eating parts of an animal. The marshmallow ingredient "gelatin" is made from animal by-products, such as bones and skin, from the meat industry. Cheese is made with rennet, an enzyme from the stomach of calves, sheep, and goats. Even honey, made by bees, is technically an animal product.

STOP AND THINK

You may eat because you're hungry or because you love the taste of a particular food. You may eat because you're bored, out of habit, or because someone tells you it's dinnertime. Maybe you chug a glass of milk, scarf down a hot dog, and pop a few cookies in your mouth for dessert without thinking much about it.

Stop and consider what you eat and why you eat it. Vegans think of how their food choices impact Earth, its people, and its animals. They've come to the conclusion that the cost of eating meat—to animals, to the environment, and to their health—is too high.

Give It Up for Veganism!

When people switch to vegetarianism or veganism, others may ask them what the hardest food was to give up. They might have a variety of answers. But many vegans don't miss a thing.

Greg has been a vegan for about a year and a half. "I honestly did not have trouble giving up any food," he says. "Everyone assumes it must be difficult, but it just wasn't."

Alyssa's been a vegan for a year. "I've pretty much found or created vegan alternatives for anything that I crave," she says.

Let's Eat

PLENTY-OF-PLANTS PIZZA

Some people celebrate Friday night with pizza. Try this colorful vegan version of a classic with lots of fresh vegetables. You can broil the vegetables indoors or grill them outside. (serves 4)

Ingredients

1 small eggplant

olive oil

salt and pepper

1 red bell pepper

½ marinated artichoke heart

about 10 pitted kalamata olives

about 6 sun dried tomato halves

1 14-ounce can diced tomatoes, drained

focaccia bread

dried basil leaves

Steps

Set oven temperature to broil.

Slice the eggplant from top to bottom into 1/2 -inch-thick slices. Brush both sides with olive oil and sprinkle with salt and pepper. Lay on a broiler pan.

Cut the pepper in half (save one half for another recipe). Lay the pepper half cut-side down on the broiler pan as well. Broil the eggplant and pepper on high for 5 minutes.

Flip the eggplant slices over. (Leave the pepper as it is.) Broil for another 5 minutes.

Take out the eggplant and set aside on a plate. Continue cooking the pepper for about 5 minutes more, or until the outside skin is completely black.

When the pepper is done, place it in a brown paper bag, and fold over the top. Let it steam in the bag for about 5 minutes. Take out the pepper, and peel off the black skin and discard. Rinse pepper under cold water. Set aside.

In a food processor, combine the artichoke heart, olives, and sun dried tomatoes. Put in a bowl. Add the drained diced tomatoes. Combine well to make a chunky sauce.

Cut the focaccia bread in half horizontally. Spread the sauce on the two flat halves of bread. Slice the eggplant into strips and lay over both halves. Slice the red pepper and place over the eggplant. Sprinkle with dried basil.

Bake at 400°F for about 10 minutes or until warmed through. Slice and serve!

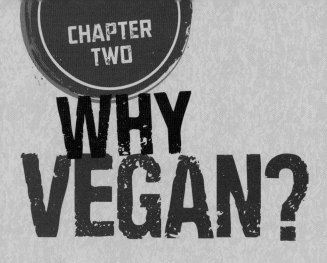

CHAPTER TWO

WHY VEGAN?

GREG STARTED AS A VEGETARIAN. AFTER EIGHT MONTHS HE WENT VEGAN. "My main reason for becoming a vegan was concern for animals," he says. "I'm driven by a belief that consuming animal products is cruel and unnecessary."

Greg started thinking about vegetarianism in high school. This idea came not from his friends but from books and poetry he read. "I learned about Gandhi in my ninth grade social studies class, so I went and bought his autobiography," he says. Mohandas Gandhi was a spiritual and political leader in India who believed in peaceful protest. "As I read, I started to view the consumption of animals as immoral." After Greg read a poem in his creative writing class, he started thinking about the food he ate. "The poem suggested that if we were forced to see how meat was produced, we would no longer be able to eat it. That made a lot of sense to me."

Picture books, television commercials, and even food packaging show idyllic farms with animals enjoying vast, sunny acres. We've been raised to believe this is what all farms are like. So we don't think twice when we have steak tips, chicken breast, or pork chops for dinner. But most conventional farms don't resemble these images. While modern farming methods aren't a secret, many people still don't know how animals are "processed" to make our food. Vegans have decided they want the truth.

Animals' flesh is butchered into various cuts, depending on which part of the animal the meat came from.

According to the American Meat Institute, in 2006 Americans ate about 234 pounds of meat per person.

COMPASSION FOR ANIMALS

Because we live in such a meat-based culture, the food industry has to supply a lot of meat. Today most animals for meat are raised on large farms called CAFOs (concentrated animal feeding operations). Some people call them factory farms because they resemble automated factories more than they resemble traditional farms. Animals are considered products to process into forms the industry can sell. A cow, pig, chicken, or turkey goes from being a living, breathing animal to plastic-wrapped meat.

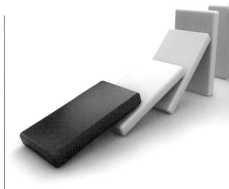

Power of One

When a problem feels overwhelming, such as world hunger, the environment, or the treatment of animals, what can one person do to make a difference? It is a question many people ask when a cause feels monumental. But there is power in one.

In America there is a large demand for meat and animal products. Companies make what customers buy. If you decide not to purchase animal products, the companies lose a customer. One customer doesn't make a huge difference. But if you share your feelings with others, they might decide to stop purchasing animal products too. And if they tell friends, and they tell friends, companies aren't just losing one customer. They would lose 10, or 100, or 1,000. Companies would notice that.

Chickens lay eggs like machines on an assembly line.

What does this mean for the animals? For cows, it means being penned-in and crowded into feedlots. Here farmers feed cows corn instead of their natural diet of grass so the animals grow fatter faster. The feed might contain antibiotics to keep disease from spreading among the crowded cows. Farmers might inject the cows with growth hormones to help them grow fast.

Male calves are sold to veal producers. Veal calves are kept in pens too small for them to move around so they don't use their muscles. Farmers want to keep the muscle meat pale and tender.

Chickens are crowded by the thousands into large sheds. Farmers keep sheds cramped so the chickens can't run around and lose weight. Today's chickens have been bred to grow to maturity in almost half the time they did in the past. Diseases spread easily in such close conditions, so they're given antibiotics.

Workers sort chicken parts from a conveyor belt.

Pigs are also kept indoors, in crowded pens with concrete floors. A mother pig is allowed to nurse her piglets, but she may be placed in a pen just big enough for her body. Metal bars force her to stay on her side. The bar prevents her from rolling onto her piglets, but also keeps her from moving or becoming comfortable.

At the end of these rushed, cramped lives, the animals are brought to a slaughterhouse. They are killed, skinned or feathered, and carved into pieces so that they can be wrapped up and sent to your supermarket.

While eggs and milk don't necessitate the killing of animals, vegans are still concerned with the treatment of the animals. Egg-laying hens may be cramped in wire cages stacked on top of each other. The cages are so tiny that hens can't even spread their wings. If they are cage-free hens, they are not caged, but they are still crowded together on a shed floor. Their waste builds up. Their beaks may be seared off so that they don't peck at each other.

Dairy cows may spend most of their lives standing on a concrete floor. They are not fed their natural grass diet, but a high-protein diet (often containing other animals and animal by-products) so that they can produce a lot of milk. Some are given hormones to increase milk production even more. Before a cow's milk can run out, she is impregnated again. When she doesn't produce well anymore, she is sent to slaughter.

Fish farming is similar to land farming. Fish are crowded by the thousands in cramped tanks or holding ponds. They are fed special pellets to make them gain weight quickly. They are given antibiotics so they don't get sick from being so close.

Not all farms treat their animals this way, of course. At smaller, local farms, cows may eat grass, and pigs and chickens are given more access to the outdoors. The animals may live longer, less stressful lives. But, in the end, they too are slaughtered for human consumption.

Vegans are concerned about how animals are treated to feed our meat-centered appetites. Vegans feel this treatment is inhumane and unnecessary when there are so many other good foods to eat.

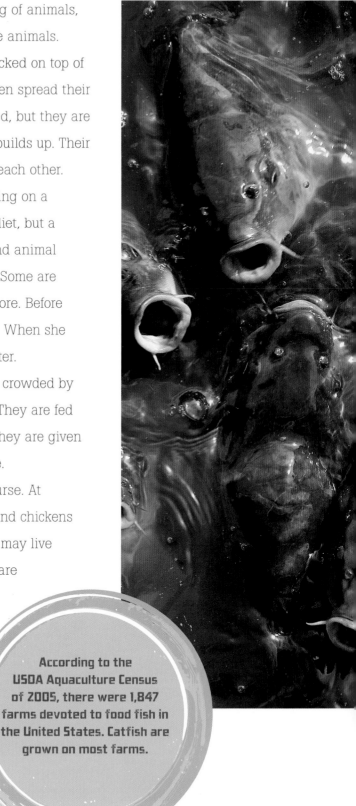

According to the USDA Aquaculture Census of 2005, there were 1,847 farms devoted to food fish in the United States. Catfish are grown on most farms.

Catfish crowd together in the tanks on a fish farm.

COMPASSION FOR PEOPLE

In the U.S. many people have food in abundance. But that's not true everywhere. World hunger is a monumental problem. The Food and Agriculture Organization of the United Nations states that the number of people in the world considered "undernourished" totals 925 million. Most of those people live in Asia and Africa. The problem gets worse as our world population increases. Did you know that every minute, about 100 people die, but about 250 people are born? This causes the population to steadily increase every day.

Most of the world's grain isn't used to feed people. It's used to feed animals. The USDA Foreign Agricultural Service stated that in 2007, more than half of the total grain consumed in the United States was fed to livestock. Many folks have chosen to go vegetarian or vegan because they believe by cutting out meat, we could feed more people.

Right: Farmers harvest wheat in Akron, Colorado.

Far right: Children deal with hunger at a refugee camp as they await aid in Somalia.

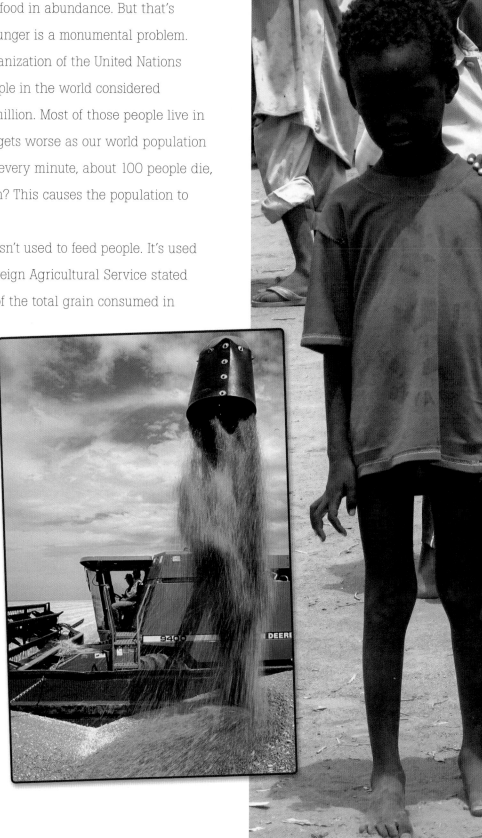

Agricultural chemicals can make their way into nearby water supplies.

COMPASSION FOR THE ENVIRONMENT

Some people choose to go vegetarian or vegan out of concern for the world's resources. The Environmental Protection Agency has cited runoff from agriculture as the leading source of pollution to rivers and lakes. And since many crops are grown just to feed animals, vegans feel avoiding meat would cut down on pollution.

Many farmers use synthetic pesticides to keep bugs away, or synthetic fertilizers to help the crops grow. These chemicals get into the soil, then into the groundwater. The groundwater makes its way into your drinking water. It also seeps into rivers and streams and can do major damage to the plants and animals that live there. Fish living in polluted waters absorb chemicals and other toxins, which become concentrated in their flesh. If you eat these fish, the toxins get into your body too.

Most freshwater in the world, about 70 percent, is used for irrigation. Immense amounts of water are needed to irrigate feed crops. All the animals in CAFOs create a lot of waste—the EPA estimates about 500 million tons of manure a year. This waste may be stored in large lagoons. In the event of a leak or heavy rainfall, waste may find its way out of a lagoon and into our water supply.

Livestock also affect the air around them. They create gas as they digest their food. These harmful greenhouse gases escape into the atmosphere and create environmental problems that may ultimately cause climate changes over the entire planet.

By removing meat from the equation, vegans hope a lot of these problems will be solved. They believe a vegan diet can help change the world.

U.S. Greenhouse Gas Emissions [2009]

in teragrams of CO_2 equivalent
(1 teragram = 1 trillion grams)

Electric Power Industry
2,193.0

Transportation
1,815.8

Industry
1,330.6

Agriculture
490.0

Commercial
404.3

Residential
360.5

U.S. Territories
45.5

TOTAL EMISSIONS
6,639.7

COMPASSION FOR YOURSELF

A vegan diet can help change you too! The American Dietetic Association has officially stated: "Appropriately planned vegetarian diets, including total vegetarian or vegan diets, are healthful, nutritionally adequate, and may provide health benefits in the prevention and treatment of certain diseases." Scientific studies have shown that a vegan diet reduces the risk of heart disease, some cancers, and certain types of diabetes.

Alyssa made the switch to veganism because "I knew that it was better for my health and that it would cause less stress on the environment. I couldn't stand the way meat industries operate. I did not want to contribute to that industry in any way."

We all have to eat. And we like to have choices. Despite what you may think, leaving out meat doesn't leave out variety or good taste. Check out the next chapter to see all the foods vegans have to choose from.

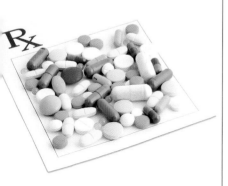

Decrease Disease

If you choose an animal-free diet, you may decrease your risk for:

HEART DISEASE

DIABETES

CANCER

HIGH BLOOD PRESSURE

KIDNEY STONES AND GALLSTONES

OSTEOPOROSIS

Let's Eat

CHILI SOUP

When you have a little more time to cook, try this tasty simmering soup. It will warm you up on a chilly or rainy night.

Ingredients

2 tablespoons olive oil

1 large yellow onion, chopped

2 cloves garlic, minced

½ of a red bell pepper, chopped

1 4-ounce can chopped green chilies

1 tablespoon chili powder

½ teaspoon cumin

½ teaspoon smoked paprika

½ teaspoon salt

½ teaspoon black pepper

1 14-ounce can diced tomatoes

2 cups vegetable broth

2 cups water

2 tablespoons tomato paste

1 14-ounce can red kidney beans, rinsed and drained

Steps

Heat the olive oil in a stockpot. Add the onion and sauté about 10 minutes on medium high until clear and browned. Add garlic, red bell pepper, and chopped green chilies. Sauté about 3 minutes more.

Add the chili powder, cumin, paprika, salt, and pepper. Cook about a minute.

Stir in the diced tomatoes (and their juices), vegetable broth, water, tomato paste, and beans.

Cover and bring to a boil. Reduce heat to low and let simmer covered for about an hour, stirring occasionally.

CHAPTER THREE

CRUELTY-FREE CUISINE

TREAT YOURSELF TO DELICIOUS FOODS. THAT'S EASY TO DO AS A VEGAN. Some people may tell you that you'll be missing out on important nutrients. But a varied, delicious vegan diet can provide all the nutrients your body needs.

Since Greg has become a vegan, he's realized how unhealthy his diet used to be. "I hardly ate any fruits, vegetables, or whole grains," he says. "When I did have vegetables, they were drowned in butter. I also ate fast food about twice a week, and drank soda every day." Greg cut out animal products and learned a lot about what it means to eat healthy.

If you decide to go vegan, be responsible. Don't embark on this new lifestyle if you're just looking for a way to lose weight. Any food choices you make should be about good health, not about reaching a certain number on a scale. Especially as a teenager, your body is changing and developing. It needs proper nutrition to grow. You may want to respect the world and the animals in it, but you also have to respect your body. Treat yourself well. Get to know what your body needs.

FEED THE NEED

Carbohydrates, protein, fat, vitamins, and minerals—these are the five nutrients your body needs to function. Here's what they do and why you need them:

Carbohydrates are the sugars and starches that give your body fuel for energy. Fiber includes carbohydrates that your body can't digest. They keep your digestive system running smoothly.

Protein provides the tools you need to grow, repair, and maintain your body tissues. Protein is made up of amino acids. There are 20 amino acids. Your body can create some itself. It gets the others from protein-rich food.

Fat stores energy, cushions your organs, and keeps you warm. Omega-3 and omega-6 fatty acids are good for you. But saturated fat (the kind that is solid at room temperature—such as butter and animal fat) is not.

Vitamins and minerals are necessary substances that help your body do a variety of jobs. Calcium builds your bones. Iron helps your body deliver oxygen to your cells. Vitamin D helps you absorb calcium. Zinc helps your immune system. Riboflavin helps you produce red blood cells. Vitamin A, vitamin C, and many other vitamins need to be a part of your diet.

Animal products provide some of the nutrients your body needs, but they do so at some risk. Meat contains protein—but it also has a lot of saturated fat and cholesterol. Fish have omega-3 fatty acids, but can also have traces of toxins from contaminated waterways. Milk has calcium, but there are plenty of other calcium sources that don't come with the added risks of growth hormones or antibiotics that may have been given to the dairy cows. Eggs have protein, but also lots of cholesterol and fat. Raw eggs also carry the risk of the bacteria salmonella that can lead to food poisoning.

Butter is a saturated fat, which means it is solid at room temperature. Olive oil and some other plant-based oils are better for your health.

Protein's Just a Part

Alyssa says that people often ask her where she gets her protein. "It's a rather silly question," she says. "There's an illusion that we need a huge amount of protein every day, and that's just not true."

Many people eat a lot more protein than they need. Expert nutritionists recommend that about 50 percent of your daily caloric intake should come from carbohydrates. Around 25 to 30 percent of your calories should be from healthy oils and fats. Protein should comprise another 25 to 30 percent. From tofu to tempeh to pumpkin seeds, vegans can choose from a wide variety of plant-based protein sources.

On the other hand, plant products have fiber. Animal products do not. Plants have less sodium and fat than animal products. And they are a great source of vitamins and minerals.

Keep in mind, however, that not all vitamins are vegan. It depends on their source. Retinol is a type of vitamin A, but it comes from animals, not plants. Carotene is also vitamin A and it's plant based. Types of vitamin D come from fish, milk, and eggs. Another place to get it? Sunshine!

There is one vitamin, B12, that's found in animal products and not in many vegan foods. It is important for vegans to include B12 in their diets through a vitamin supplement and through milk substitutes, cereals, or other fortified foods.

Be sure to let your doctor know if you've decided to go vegan. Show him or her that you've done your research. He or she will be able to make sure you're growing and getting all the nutrients you need. If there is concern you're missing something, he or she can recommend a supplement. Ashley consulted her doctor. "She

Let your doctor know if you decide to go vegan so he or she can give you advice.

Check out doctor-recommended sources of information for vegans and to learn more about how diet is related to overall health.

was supportive," Ashley says. "She just reminded me to keep an eye on what I ate."

Peanut butter and other nut butters (such as cashew or almond) are great sources of protein at lunch or snack time.

WHERE TO GET THE GOOD STUFF

You don't have to look far for your nutrients. Here's where you can get the good stuff:

Grains, such as wheat, corn, millet, barley, bulgur, and rice, are full of carbohydrates. You'll find grains in bread, pasta, crackers, cereal, tortillas, and popcorn. Try to eat whole grains whenever you can. Whole grains use the entire grain seed, called a kernel. Refined grains are missing part of the kernel. They're missing some vitamins and minerals too. Whole grains also contain fiber, protein, vitamins, and minerals. Cereals and breads are sometimes fortified with extra vitamins and minerals, including iron and B12.

Nuts and seeds are great protein sources, and there are plenty to choose from. Peanuts, cashews, walnuts, and pecans are just a few snacks you can easily take along with you. Pumpkin seeds and sunflower seeds are great to sprinkle on salads or other dishes. Besides protein, nuts contain healthy fats, such as the omega-3 found in flaxseed and walnuts.

Try It, You'll Like It!
Try these substitutes instead of the traditional options.

instead of this ...	try this ...
red meat, pork, poultry, fish	beans, lentils, tofu, tempeh, nuts, "fake" meats
milk	soy milk, nut milks, rice milk
cheese	soy- and nut-based alternatives
eggs	scrambled tofu, powdered egg replacements
butter	vegan dairy-free spreads

A Vegan Day

According to the newest food guidelines from the USDA, vegans should eat the following per day (based on a diet of 2,400 calories a day):

Fruit → 2 cups

Vegetables → 3 cups

Grains → 8 ounces

Protein → 6.5 ounces

Dairy [vegan] → 3 cups

Oils → 21 grams

Legumes are the "meatiest" of vegan foods. This category includes beans, peas, and lentils. They are good replacements for meat protein and can easily be the basis for a meal. Cook them into a stir fry, a soup, or a pasta dish. They also contain carbohydrates, fiber, iron, calcium, and vitamins. Look for many varieties in cans and bags, such as red pinto beans, white navy beans, black-eyed peas, chickpeas, soybeans, and many more.

Fruit means fiber! You can eat it fresh, frozen, canned, or dried. Fruit also contains carbohydrate sugars. These more natural sugars are better for your body than added sugars in packaged foods. Why not try some fruits you've never had before? Snack on pomegranate seeds, a good source of antioxidants, or figs, which provide an excellent dose of calcium.

Vegetables contain vitamins, minerals, and fiber. You can find calcium in dark green leafy veggies, such as spinach, collards, and kale. Dark yellow and orange vegetables, such as carrots, sweet potatoes, and pumpkin, have healthy beta-carotene.

Legumes come in all shapes, colors, and sizes!

THE SAME THING EVEN BETTER

Are you feeling a little down about saying good-bye to ice cream, cheese, hot dogs, lunch meat, or bacon bits? Thanks to soy, you don't have to say farewell! Soybeans, a type of legume, can be made into all sorts of vegan alternatives.

Soy versions of dairy products are getting more and more common on grocery store shelves. You can find soy milk, yogurt, cheese, and ice cream. Soy is also made into a soft bean curd called tofu, or fermented into a firmer form called tempeh. Both can replace meat in many recipes. You can also eat soybeans in their bean form, called edamame. Pop them right into your mouth for a snack!

Soy is made into meat alternatives too. You can purchase soy versions of bacon, hot dogs, chicken, ribs, ground beef, and deli meats. Some taste really close to the originals. Meat alternatives can also be made out of seitan, a product derived from wheat.

Scrambled tofu looks a lot like scrambled eggs.

"CHICKEN" CURRY

Try using "fake" chicken in this recipe with an international flair. (serves 4)

Ingredients

2 tablespoons olive oil

1 small onion, chopped

2 celery stalks, chopped

Salt and pepper to taste

3 tablespoons white flour

1 tablespoon curry powder

1 14-ounce can (about 2 cups) vegetable broth

¼ cup coconut milk

2 large potatoes, peeled and diced

1 6-ounce package "chicken style" veggie strips

Steps

In a large skillet, heat the olive oil. Add the onion and celery. Cook for about 10 minutes until onions are clear and slightly browned.

Add the salt, pepper, flour, and curry powder. Stir to combine and heat for another 2 minutes.

Add the vegetable broth, milk, and potatoes. Bring to a boil. Turn down the heat, and simmer covered for 10 minutes, stirring often as the sauce thickens. Add in the veggie strips and heat about 3 to 5 minutes more.

Serve over rice.

GO FOR
THE GOAL

ARE YOU THE TYPE WHO LIKES TO JUMP RIGHT IN? OR DO YOU TAKE YOUR TIME? You can take the same approach to make the transition to veganism. But first it might help to take a look at your current eating habits.

How often do you eat meat? Does your typical breakfast include bacon and eggs, or a bowl of oatmeal and fresh fruit? You may find that a lot of your meals are already vegan, or at least vegetarian. If so, cutting out animal products may not be too difficult. But if you find most of your meals include meat, you'll have to take some time to come up with alternatives.

Take a moment to think about your favorite foods. Some of the crackers, cookies, or other packaged foods you eat may be vegan without you even realizing it. Check online for resources and lists of vegan products. If your favorite foods are popcorn shrimp, sausage, or cheese curls, you'll have to focus more energy on looking for vegan versions.

SHOPPING VEGAN

You may find some vegan foods in your local grocery store—in the produce section for fruits and vegetables, the bean aisle for legumes, the snack area for nuts, or the dairy section for soy milk alternatives. Some stores have natural food aisles devoted to healthy, organic, or vegetarian foods, or refrigerated sections with vegetarian meat alternatives or frozen vegan dinners. If a food isn't labeled vegan, be sure to read the label to check for milk products, eggs, or other animal ingredients.

You'll probably find it easier to shop at a health or natural food store that specializes in vegetarian and vegan products. Have fun experimenting with new flavors. Don't be afraid to try something new—tempeh, seitan, or quinoa (pronounced keen-wah).

Farm stands and farmers markets are great places to buy fresh produce when it's in season. Even in the busiest of cities, you can often find a market where farmers from surrounding areas make the trip to bring produce right to you.

Quinoa (left) looks like a grain, but it is actually a seed. Try it as a side dish instead of rice. Most health food stores will have quinoa and lots of other vegan products.

STEP BY STEP

It can be hard to switch from meat eater to vegan overnight. Get out the calendar and set a realistic goal. Take it step by step. Maybe try vegetarianism for a month and see how it goes. Get used to reading labels and seeking out alternatives to the foods you're used to eating. Then start cutting out foods with all animal products. Drop a few each week. Maybe within another month, you'll be vegan!

Many vegans transition over months or even years. Alyssa decided to go vegetarian when she was only 8. She didn't go vegan until she was 17—almost 10 years later. "The change was very gradual," she says. "I weeded things out from my vegetarian diet, going from milk to soy milk, butter to Earth Balance, and finally eggs to Ener-G when I declared myself a vegan."

It's OK to give yourself time to make the switch.

You can go vegan gradually. Drop animal products and add vegan alternatives a few at a time.

You Make the Rules

As a vegan, you may choose to be a label-reader who researches any and every little ingredient. Or you can not worry so much about all the little ingredients, and focus on the bigger ones instead. Make your own set of "rules" and keep them in mind when you're shopping or eating out.

But don't beat yourself up if you make a mistake. It happens to everyone. Greg reads labels and cooks his own meals, but mistakes still happen. "I can still remember eating pasta with a store-bought marinara sauce and thinking it tasted funny," he says. "When I re-read the ingredients and it said that it contained cheese, I was really grossed out."

Sometimes your body gets so used to eating animal-free that it will tell you when you've made a mistake. Alyssa remembers a time when her body fought back. "Once on the way home from a vacation, my family and I went to dinner," she remembers. "I accidentally ate vegetables sautéed with butter. Just a little while later I started getting sick. Needless to say it was not a fun car ride home!"

Culture and Religion

Some cultures and religions forbid eating certain kinds of meat. If you are Jewish or Muslim, you may not eat pork. If you are Hindu, you may not eat beef. Lots of Asian cuisine centers on tofu or vegetables instead of meat. If you're already a part of these cultures or religions, the transition to veganism might be easier for you.

GETTING THE PARENTS ON BOARD

When you tell your family you want to go vegan, their first question will probably be "why?" Be able to state your reasons clearly. Explain to them your concerns for animals, the environment, or your health. Your parents or guardian will want to be sure you're getting the proper nutrition. So be sure

According to a 2008 study by *Vegetarian Times* magazine, 3.2 percent of adults follow a vegetarian-based diet, and about 0.5 percent of them are vegan.

Offer to help the adults in your family who do the shopping and cooking. It will make the transition to veganism easier for you and them.

to explain to them what your sources for protein, carbohydrates, and vitamins will be. The more you tell them, the better they will understand your decision. And they'll be impressed that you've done your homework!

Your choice to go vegan will also affect the adults and siblings that you share meals with. Unless they all decide to go vegan with you, it could be a challenge for the main shopper or cook in your family to suit everyone's needs. So you may also have to think of ways to compromise. Help brainstorm meals your family already enjoys that can be served in the traditional way and a vegan way. Maybe instead of pasta with meatballs, you just have the red sauce instead. When dinner is burgers on the grill, toss on a portobello mushroom cap or a veggie burger for yourself.

Suggest meals that would be easy to change to vegan. For example, use vegetable broth instead of beef broth in soups, sprinkle vegan cheese and soy pepperoni instead of regular cheese and pepperoni on a pizza, or add soy milk instead of regular milk to a creamy pasta recipe. Also try to have simple quick-to-whip-up recipes on hand, besides just a peanut butter and jelly sandwich, for nights the rest of your family is eating meat.

What's the best way to control what you eat for meals? Get to know your kitchen! Tie on an apron, and learn to cook. Offer to make dinner for the family one or two nights a week. You'll get cooking practice, and maybe you can convince them how delicious eating vegan can be.

Brown Bag Ideas

Your school cafeteria probably doesn't have a special line for vegans. So brown bag it! Here are some ideas for vegan sandwiches to pack and take along.

GRILLED ZUCCHINI AND ROASTED RED PEPPER

PEANUT BUTTER (OR ANY NUT BUTTER) AND JELLY

SLICED AVOCADO, SLICED TOMATO, BEAN SPROUTS, AND "FAKE" BACON

VEGAN LUNCH MEAT SLICES AND SOY CHEESE

HUMMUS AND SLICED CUCUMBER

Learning to cook is a good way to experiment with vegan dishes and share them with your family and friends.

To have a successful night out, check online menus ahead of time. Remember to check for side dishes to make into a meal, and never be afraid to ask your server for other options.

Vegans can still go out to eat with their nonvegan friends. Sometimes it requires a little research to find restaurants that can accommodate everyone.

OUT AND ABOUT

It's much easier to control your food when you're purchasing and preparing it yourself. But it's fun to take a night off and eat out from time to time too.

If you go to a restaurant, be ready. Thai, Indian, or Japanese restaurants may already have vegan options for you. Check out the menus of other restaurants ahead of time online to see their vegan possibilities. You can call ahead to see if the restaurant

Make a Quick Reference Vegan Notebook

Make yourself a notebook to organize the information you collect about veganism. Then you'll have it handy for quick reference. You might include sections on:

RECIPES

ANIMAL INGREDIENT LISTS

VEGAN COMPANIES/FOODS

SAMPLE MENUS FOR THE WEEK

VEGAN RESTAURANTS AND THEIR MENUS

can accommodate you. When you get there, look for main dishes that can be easily adapted. If that doesn't seem possible, look at the side dishes and think about how you can make a meal of them. Don't be afraid to ask your server if something is cooked with animal products or if the chef can prepare something off the menu. On road trips, when you know you'll be making a pit stop for lunch, pack your own instead of having to face the limited options at the fast-food counter.

Keep in mind, though, that even seemingly vegan dishes at a restaurant may still have animal products, depending on how they are prepared. For example, French fries are often cooked in vegetable oil but still may have some beef flavoring. A salad dressing may contain anchovies. Rice may be cooked in chicken broth. Your sautéed vegetables may be cooked in butter or on the same grill or pan that cooked meat. You decide where you draw the line of what's acceptable to you.

Greg says, "When I eat at a restaurant that's not specifically vegan, there's always a chance my food contains dairy or eggs, or was cooked in the same oil or pan as a meat dish. I ask before I order, but I know that it's bound to happen sometimes. I just stay positive and don't worry about it."

Probably the safest bet is to seek out vegetarian and vegan restaurants in your area. They understand you and your needs. They are great places to ask questions, get recipe ideas, try new flavors, and meet other vegans. Ask the people there for tips and advice. They'll probably be very willing to share what they've learned about veganism with you.

IT MAY NOT BE EASY

You want to be respected for your decision. But some vegans discover that their families don't support their choice. They may say, "You're just going through a phase." They may even criticize you.

You can stand up for what you believe in, but respect others' opinions too. Share your reasons for going vegan in a way that doesn't make listeners feel bad about their choices. By keeping a positive attitude, you'll be living proof that veganism is an excellent, healthy choice.

Restaurants may not use separate pans to cook meat and vegetables. Ask your server if you're concerned. Or stick to vegetarian restaurants that don't cook meat at all.

Alyssa tries hard not to judge other people's eating habits. "I never try to force my beliefs on those around me," she says. "I present logical arguments to those who want to debate with me, but I would never be so crass as to disregard a person on a single personal choice."

No matter how positive you try to be, people may still criticize you. Greg knew that his family wouldn't agree with his choice. "I knew my family wouldn't support my decision. I felt powerless because my parents controlled what food was purchased and what we ate for meals." So Greg researched veganism in high school. But then he waited until after he was out of school and on his own to make the change.

It's OK to wait. Collect the information now. Then you'll feel empowered to make the change when you decide the time is right.

Don't rush into a decision to go vegan. You can take your time to make the switch.

ZUCCHINI CHIPS

Who doesn't like chips and dip? If you're having friends over, bake up these crispy zucchini chips. One dip, and your friends will agree that veganism can be really tasty.

Ingredients

vegetable cooking spray

1 cup plain bread crumbs

½ cup white flour

½ cup soy milk

½ teaspoon salt

¼ teaspoon black pepper

½ teaspoon garlic powder

1 tablespoon parsley

1 medium-sized zucchini

marinara sauce

Steps

Spray a cookie sheet with nonstick vegetable cooking spray. Set aside.

Preheat oven to 425°F.

Set up your flour, soymilk, and bread crumbs as follows:

Put the flour into a large zippered bag. Pour the soymilk into a bowl. Combine the bread crumbs, salt, pepper, garlic powder, and parsley on a large plate. Set the flour, soy milk, and bread crumbs aside.

Cut the zucchini into thin rounds, about ⅛-inch thick.

Place all of the rounds into the bag of flour. Shake until all of the chips are well-coated.

One by one, dip a chip into the soymilk. Then dip it into the bread crumbs. Repeat with all the chips and lay them in a single layer on the cookie sheet.

Spray the tops of all the chips with cooking spray.

Bake for 10 minutes.

Flip with a turner. Bake another 10 minutes. Flip them again, and bake 3 to 5 minutes more, until browned and crispy.

Dip in your favorite marinara sauce.

CHAPTER FIVE

MORE THAN JUST MEALS

VEGANISM ISN'T JUST ABOUT WHAT YOU EAT FOR BREAKFAST, LUNCH, AND DINNER. For most vegans it's a lifestyle change that affects all areas of their lives.

ANIMALS IN THE CLOSET

Look in the closet. Do you have shoes or a jacket made of leather? Wool sweaters and mittens? A silk blouse or scarf? Anything made from fur? Check out your bed. Do you have pillows and a comforter made of down? All of these are animal products.

Slaughterhouses send their animal skins to the leather industry to be made into jackets, purses, boots, belts, and wallets. Wool is sheared off of sheep. Silk is made from the cocoon threads from silkworms. Fur, of course, can come from a variety of mammals. Down is feathers plucked from a goose.

There are many other choices for vegans. Most alternatives are synthetic, such as pleather, faux fur, nylon, polyester, fleece, rayon, and synthetic down. These options are often a lot cheaper than animal fabrics.

Some vegans are concerned that synthetic alternatives may cause harm to the environment, because they are plastic-based. While fleece is made of plastic, it is often made from recycled plastic bottles, so it can help cut down on waste. But there are natural clothing alternatives too. Cotton comes from plants. Canvas is thicker cotton used for shoes. Tencel is made from wood pulp.

Alyssa has found great places to shop for animal-friendly shoes. But she's had more trouble finding nonleather sports equipment. "Avoiding leather is a big problem since I'm a softball player," she says. "I have to use a leather glove because there are so few alternatives out there."

ANIMALS IN THE BATHROOM

Look in the bathroom. There are lots of products that may have animal ingredients too. Read the label on your hand cream. Does it contain lanolin? Lanolin is an animal product—an oil found on wooly animals' hair. Beeswax may be an ingredient in your lip balm. Your perfume might have musk. Many soaps are made with animal fats. Shampoos may contain keratin to strengthen your hair. You might use a hairbrush with boar bristles, or a makeup brush made of sable hair. All of these are animal ingredients. Vegans try to avoid them and look for plant-based or synthetic versions instead. Some

Animal products are found in many health and beauty items people use every day.

clothing materials
vegans may avoid

mohair
(from goats)

silk
(from silkworms)

wool
(from sheep)

angora
(from rabbit or goat)

cashmere, pashmina
(from goats)

fur
(from mink, fox, rabbits, and others)

down
(from geese or ducks)

leather, suede, calfskin, sheepskin, shearling, alligator skin, snake skin
(from a variety of animals)

other ingredients
vegans may avoid

beeswax
(from bees)

bone meal
(from animal bones)

lanolin
(from wool)

carmine/cochineal
(a red dye that comes from beetles)

catgut
(from intestines of sheep and horses)

gelatin
(made from animal by-products)

glycerin
(by-product of soap manufacturing)

stearic acid
(fat from a variety of animals)

musk
(from a variety of animals)

keratin
(from the horns, hooves, feathers, quills, and hair of animals)

And more ... Check online sources for a full list.

Don't keep it a secret! Avoid uncomfortable food situations by letting people know you're a vegan.

ingredients can be from either animal or plant sources. Just as with other aspects of your vegan lifestyle, it is up to you where you want to set your limits.

Some cosmetic, perfume, and cleaning product companies test products on rabbits, mice, or other small animals to see if they are safe for people to use. The animals can be hurt and even killed in the process. Many companies have banned these tests. Often their labels clearly state "Cruelty-free" or "We do not test on animals." If you're not sure, contact the company to find out.

When Greg decided to go vegan, he had fun cleaning out his closet and bathroom cabinets. "I went through and replaced all of my clothes and other products with ones made without animal ingredients and without animal testing."

STAND UP FOR YOUR CHOICE

If you keep your veganism a secret, you may put yourself in an uncomfortable situation. What happens when Grandma buys you a new down jacket for Christmas? Or a friend makes you a cake for your birthday but didn't know you avoid eggs? You can speak out for what's important to you.

If you're invited to a friend's house for dinner, let them know you're a vegan before you get there. That way you won't offend your hosts by not eating what they've prepared. Large family gatherings can present a challenge for a few reasons, especially around the holidays. Alyssa remembers one Thanksgiving: "It was really weird being the only non-meat eater at a holiday dinner based around a huge slab of meat." She solved the problem by bringing along her vegan version of the meal—fake turkey—so she could join the festivities but not have to compromise her vegan choices.

Build Your Own Support System

If you don't have someone in your family to turn to for support, look to your community. Perhaps you can start a club at school and pass out literature (or tasty vegan cookies) to help spread the word. Or look for local groups that will support your new lifestyle with tips and ideas. Maybe start at a local vegetarian restaurant to see what community connections are available to you.

Gatherings can also be a challenge when your family or relatives don't support you. In these situations Greg has found that certain people tease him or make rude comments about his choice to go vegan. Even though he has a positive message, Greg says, "They sense their way of life is being attacked and they need to prove why veganism is wrong."

You can't control what people think of your choices. But you can control your reaction to it. Stay positive. Show others that you've decided veganism is worth the trouble for a more compassionate world. Greg's veganism makes him feel optimistic and empowered. "The world is filled with so many problems; it can be overwhelming and depressing. But I know that people have the power to affect positive change."

Check online for vegan recipes and tips to share with family and friends.

SWEET TREAT VEGAN COOKIES

You don't need butter and eggs to make cookies. Try baking up these sweet treats to share with friends. (Makes about 2 dozen cookies.)

Ingredients

¾ cup vegan margarine

½ cup maple syrup

½ cup brown sugar

½ cup almond butter (or peanut butter)

½ teaspoon vanilla extract

1 cup white flour

1 cup whole wheat flour

1 cup oats

1 ½ teaspoons baking soda

½ cup vegan chocolate chips

½ teaspoon cinnamon

1 tablespoon white sugar

1 tablespoon wheat germ

Steps

Preheat oven to 350°F.

In a large bowl, blend together the margarine, syrup, brown sugar, almond butter, and vanilla until smooth.

In a small bowl, combine the flours, oats, and baking soda. Add to the bowl of wet ingredients and mix well. Stir in the chocolate chips.

On a plate combine the cinnamon, white sugar, and wheat germ.

Form the dough into 1-inch balls. Roll each ball in the cinnamon mixture.

Place on a cookie sheet about 2-inches apart. Bake for about 10 minutes.

METRIC CONVERSIONS

TEMPERATURE

Degrees Fahrenheit	Degrees Celsius
250	120
300	150
350	180
375	190
400	200
425	220

WEIGHT

United States	Metric
1 ounce	30 grams
½ pound	225 grams
1 pound	455 grams

VOLUME

United States	Metric
¼ teaspoon	1.2 milliliters
½ teaspoon	2.5 milliliters
1 teaspoon	5 milliliters
1 tablespoon	15 milliliters
¼ cup	60 milliliters
⅓ cup	80 milliliters
½ cup	120 milliliters
1 cup	240 milliliters
1 quart	1 liter

GLOSSARY

by-product something produced in the process of making something else

emission a substance that is released into the air

enzyme a substance that produces a chemical change

fortified containing added nutritional ingredients

groundwater water found in underground chambers; it is tapped for drinking water through wells and springs

irrigate to supply with water

manure animal waste used as fertilizer

nutrient a substance in food that a body needs to grow and function

organic processed in a more natural way to help conserve the health of land, animals, and crops

pesticide a chemical used to kill insects or small animals

runoff substances that flow into rivers and streams

supplement an extra source of a vitamin or mineral

synthetic artificial, not natural

toxin a substance that is harmful or poisonous

undernourished not receiving enough food or nutrients for proper growth

READ MORE

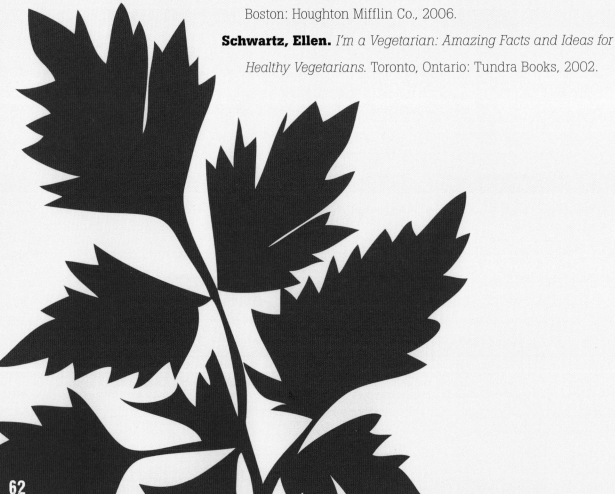

Kneidel, Sally, and Sara Kate Kneidel. *Veggie Revolution: Smart Choices for a Healthy Body and a Healthy Planet.* Golden, Colo.: Fulcrum Pub., 2005.

McCann, Jennifer. *Vegan Lunch Box: 130 Amazing, Animal-Free Lunches Kids and Grown-ups Will Love!* Cambridge, Mass.: DaCapo Lifelong, 2008.

Raymond, Carole. *Student's Go Vegan Cookbook: Over 135 Quick, Easy, Cheap, and Tasty Vegan Recipes.* New York: Three Rivers Press, 2006.

Schlosser, Eric, and Charles Wilson. *Chew on This: Everything You Don't Want to Know about Fast Food.* Boston: Houghton Mifflin Co., 2006.

Schwartz, Ellen. *I'm a Vegetarian: Amazing Facts and Ideas for Healthy Vegetarians.* Toronto, Ontario: Tundra Books, 2002.

INTERNET SITES

Use *FactHound* to find Internet sites related to this book. All of the sites on *FactHound* have been researched by our staff.

Here's all you do:

Visit *www.facthound.com*

Type in this code: **9780756545215**

ABOUT THE AUTHOR

Dana Meachen Rau has written more than 300 books for children and teens, including cookbooks that encourage healthy, thoughtful eating. She visits farm stands, tends her garden, and makes meals with her family in Burlington, Connecticut.

INDEX